BONSAI

FOREWORD *Luigi Crespi*

PHOTOGRAPHS *Fabio Petroni*

TEXT *Anna Maria Botticelli*

COORDINATION *Susanna Crespi*

Editorial production *Valeria Manferto De Fabianis*

Graphic design *Marinella Debernardi*

"Contents"

CRESPI
BONSAI
MUSEUM

IN COLLABORATION WITH
CRESPI BONSAI MUSEUM

"Through bonsai, I discovered the spirit of trees"

THE FIRST APPROACH TO BONSAI OFTEN HAPPENS PARTLY BY CHANCE, PARTLY THROUGH CURIOSITY, BUT ALSO BECAUSE YOU ALREADY LOVE NATURE AND WANT TO FIND OUT ABOUT EVERY ASPECT. AND THEN THIS INCREDIBLE WORLD ENDS UP INFLUENCING THE ENTIRE COURSE OF YOUR LIFE. THIS IS HOW IT WAS FOR ME.

WHEN YOU DECIDE TO TAKE UP THE ART OF BONSAI, YOU EMBARK ON A GENUINE JOURNEY WHICH WILL BRING YOU NEW EXPERIENCES AND NEW KNOWLEDGE ABOUT THE ASPECTS AND CHARACTERISTICS OF A WORLD SO DISTANT, BUT IN FACT SO NEAR-AT-HAND. BECAUSE NATURE HAS ALWAYS BELONGED TO US, OR PERHAPS IT IS ACTUALLY WE WHO BELONG TO NATURE. I BELIEVE THIS PRIMORDIAL NECESSITY TO DEVOTE OURSELVES TO TREES, WITHOUT WHICH WE WOULD BE UNABLE TO LIVE ON THE EARTH, IS AN INNATE NEED.

I CONSIDER MYSELF A LUCKY MAN, I DON'T DENY IT. BONSAI HAVE ENABLED ME TO DISCOVER THE SPIRIT OF TREES, A JOURNEY COVERED BY DEGREES, IN SMALL SOMETIMES DIFFICULT STEPS, BUT ALL THE MORE THRILLING AND FULL OF SATISFACTION PRECISELY BECAUSE OF THAT.

TENDING BONSAI IS MORE THAN JUST AN ART. IT IS ALSO A PHILOSOPHY OF LIFE, IT IS PURE PASSION, IT IS DIRECT CONTACT WITH THE WORLD OF PLANTS, BECAUSE THE BONSAI IS A LIVING AND CONSTANTLY TRANSFORMING WORK OF ART, GIVING US A CLOSE-UP VIEW OF THE CHANGING SEASONS... AND EVERY CHANGE BRINGS NEW EMOTIONS.

WHEN THEY SUGGESTED I WROTE ABOUT THE PLANTS IN THE COLLECTION I KEEP HERE AT THE CRESPI BONSAI MUSEUM, I WAS AFRAID MY LIFE COMPANIONS WOULD BE MISREPRESENTED AND WOULD LOSE ALL THEIR MEANING FOR ME, THEIR VITALITY AND THEIR MAGIC.

THE LAST THING I WANTED WAS A BOOK-CATALOGUE AND WHEN THE CREATOR OF THE EXCEPTIONAL PHOTOGRAPHS IN THIS BOOK, FABIO PETRONI, PROMISED HE WOULD BRING MY PLANTS TO LIFE ON THE BLANK PAGES, I FOLLOWED MY INTUITION, JUST AS I HAVE ALWAYS DONE THROUGHOUT MY LIFE. I TOOK HIM AT HIS WORD. I WAS NOT WRONG AND I AM TRULY DELIGHTED.

THE EMOTIONS WHICH WASH OVER YOU WHEN YOU OBSERVE A BONSAI HAVE BEEN BRILLIANTLY TRANSLATED INTO WORDS BY ANNA MARIA BOTTICELLI, THE SPLENDID AUTHOR OF THE TEXT WHICH ACCOMPANIES MY BONSAI.

THE BEAUTY OF THE BONSAI IS FOR ME A REFUGE FOR THE SOUL, BRINGING WITH IT AN APPRECIATION OF THE SILENT BREATHING OF NATURE. I HOPE THAT WHEN YOU HAVE BROWSED THROUGH AND READ THIS BOOK, YOU WILL SHARE THIS THOUGHT.

LUIGI CRESPI

When you observe an old bonsai, you cannot help but be fascinated by the patina which surrounds it. The passage of time leaves traces which relate its history... and the longer the time, the deeper the traces. Its history is told through the trunk, the branches and the bark. As they grow older, they acquire shapes and colours both inimitable and continuously changing under the constant influence of the slow flowing of time. A bonsai reveals its essence through its perfect structure, sometimes so perfect and balanced that it can no longer be considered as merely a tree in a pot, but a genuine work of art. And when the artist successfully achieves perfection in his creation, it is as though the works of art were created by Mother Nature, rather than by the hand of man.

I believe this is the right description for the trees you will meet on the following pages.

I was brought up on books and bonsai, a strange combination when you think that to make a book, you need a tree. But maybe not so strange if you consider the common destiny which sometimes binds a book and a tree together. In the hands of a good collector, a book can pass undamaged down the years, if not the centuries. In the same way, if lovingly tended, a bonsai can reach hundreds of years.

Housed in the Crespi Bonsai Museum (part of the prestigious circuit of Great Italian Gardens), all the trees selected for this book have been created by the sometimes internationally famous artists who have written the history of bonsai. Artists who have successfully avoided distracting attention away from their works, as this is the only way to comprehend the origin of the tree in which the universe is revealed

"*After all this time, it still surprises me*"

AND THE LAWS OF ITS NATURE ARE EXPRESSED. THE TRUE ARTIST DOES NOT PAY EXCESSIVE ATTENTION TO OUTWARD APPEARANCES, OR TO WHAT HE MUST CREATE WITH THEM. THE EXTERNAL FORM IS NOT HIS PRIMARY OBJECTIVE, BUT RATHER A MEANS THROUGH WHICH TO EXTRAPOLATE THE SOUL OF THE TREE AND PRESENT IT TO THE OBSERVER.

WHEN YOU ADMIRE A BONSAI, YOU OFTEN FEEL AS THOUGH CATAPULTED INTO A PARALLEL WORLD. YOU ARE LOOKING AT A TREE THAT IN NATURE WOULD REACH A HEIGHT OF, PERHAPS, AS MUCH AS 30-40 M (98-131 FT). AND THERE IT IS IN FRONT OF YOU, ENCLOSED IN A SMALL POT. AFTER ALL THIS TIME, IT STILL SURPRISES ME.

CREATING A BONSAI WITH THESE CHARACTERISTICS IS EXTREMELY DIFFICULT, BUT IT IS EVEN MORE DIFFICULT TO BRING IT TO LIFE THROUGH A BOOK, EVEN IF PRINTED WELL. IT TAKES MUCH MORE THAN GOOD PRINTING! IT TAKES A METICULOUS EYE. IT TAKES A PARTICULAR SENSITIVITY.

WHILE FOR PEOPLE, THE EYES ARE THE WINDOW OF THE SOUL, FOR TREES, IT IS THE SLENDER BRANCHES, THE TENDER LEAVES JUST UNFOLDED, THE INTRICATE TRUNK, THE SOFT CUSHION OF MOSS RESTING ON THE SURFACE.

THE TREES IN THE CRESPI BONSAI MUSEUM (LIKE MEMBERS OF MY FAMILY TO ME) MOVE THOSE WHO OBSERVE THEM AND AROUSE THEIR RESPECT, PARTICULARLY CONSIDERING HOW TRANSITORY AND CHANGEABLE THEY ARE, MAKING EACH MOMENT SPENT WITH THEM UNIQUE. IF THIS THOUGHT CROSSES YOUR MIND EVEN FOR JUST AN INSTANT AS YOU BROWSE THROUGH THIS BOOK, THEN WE WILL HAVE ACHIEVED OUR OBJECTIVE, WE WILL HAVE SUCCESSFULLY BROUGHT OUR BONSAI TO LIFE, THROUGH THE UNIQUE PHOTOS OF FABIO PETRONI, ACCOMPANIED BY THE STORIES OF ANNA MARIA BOTTICELLI WHO RELATES THE HISTORY OF THESE TREES IN HER INIMITABLE STYLE.

SUSANNA CRESPI

"I am a lucky man!
I always photograph beautiful worlds"

I'm an "allotment man" myself, so I entered the bonsai world on tiptoes. But when I got to know the Crespi family and visited their museum, I immediately changed approach – although I never stopped addressing all the bonsai with respect, given they were all much older than me.

During the "casting," while Susanna was telling me about each bonsai and Mr Crespi stupefied me with his silences, I experienced the strangest sensations. I was aware of the energy they emanated, they caressed me with their fascination, I was enraptured by their proportions, their beauty and their strength.

It was like finding yourself face to face with a Roman legion commanded by a beautiful woman... you have no choice but to surrender.

I kept on looking at them and studying them, then when Mr Crespi said : "I've never seen anyone looking at bonsai like you do," I realised I was on the right track.

I love nature deeply and I like feeling small in her presence. I love the way nature makes me feel both powerful and defenceless.

The bonsai is small (but are you sure?) and man is big (but are you sure?) and I wanted to restore the proportions of my philosophy. To do this, I imagined I had lost my way among the maples, sequoias and bonsai woods, with the possibility of seeing what a bird sees as it flies through the branches at a height of 30 m (98 ft) – something we humans can only imagine.

I tried to transmit everything I felt on the set in front of these trees... beauty, fascination, harmony and strength. For me, the bonsai is strength.

I can perfectly understand the samurai who meditated in front of their bonsai before a battle.

This book is part of my journey photographing nature, trying to be nature, not simply a spectator of the beautiful. Nature uses beauty to enchant, to court animals, pollens etc... to grow and to reproduce. Nature is used to the beautiful, a beauty which is not an end in itself, just like the great artists who have always used beauty and elegance to communicate and grow.

I am a lucky man! I always photograph beautiful worlds.

FABIO PETRONI

"The bonsai, to each its season"

THE WORLD OF THE BONSAI IS FASCINATING, ALLURING AND AT THE SAME TIME STILL MYSTERIOUS, MADE OF LIVING TREES KEPT SMALL BY THE EXPERT HAND OF MAN. TREES WHICH CAN REACH A GREAT AGE OF TENS, IF NOT HUNDREDS, OF YEARS AND ALTHOUGH TRAINED IN A POT AND GROWN ON A BALCONY OR IN A GARDEN, ARE STILL ABLE TO TRANSMIT THE SAME MAJESTY, ENERGY, GRACEFULNESS AND ELEGANCE AS THEY WOULD IN NATURE. BUT WHY DEDICATE A BOOK TO BONSAI? FOR TWO REASONS: FIRSTLY BECAUSE THE BONSAI SYMBOLISES JAPANESE CULTURE WHICH, MORE THAN ANY OTHER, APPRECIATES THE BEAUTY OF THE FLOW OF THE SEASONS AND EXPRESSES IT THROUGH BONSAI; SECONDLY BECAUSE THE CRESPI BONSAI MUSEUM WHICH OPENED ITS DOORS IN ITALY IN THE OUTSKIRTS OF MILAN IN 1991 IS THE WORLD'S FIRST PERMANENT BONSAI MUSEUM WHERE THE PHOTOGRAPHS OF THE LIVING MASTERPIECES MOST REPRESENTATIVE OF A UNIQUE COLLECTION WERE TAKEN.

HOW IMPORTANT THE SEASONS ARE IN JAPAN! WE TOO IN THE WEST (AND NOT ONLY THOSE OF US WITH A PASSION FOR BONSAI) FEEL REGENERATED BY THE SIGHT OF THE FIRST FLOWERS WHICH OPEN IN THE SPRING. WE LONG TO EXPOSE OUR SKIN TO THE SUN DURING THE SUMMER AND TRY AND SATISFY OUR BODY'S NEED TO REDUCE TO A MINIMUM THE RESPONSE TO EXTERNAL STIMULI WHEN THE HOURS OF LIGHT GROW SHORTER AS WINTER ADVANCES.

IN JAPANESE CULTURE, THE BONSAI IS A GLIMPSE OF THE LANDSCAPE WHICH TO THE EYES OF THE OBSERVER CHANGES CONSTANTLY ACCORDING TO THE SEASONS. IT IS DOWN TO EACH INDIVIDUAL SPECIES TO THROW OPEN A WINDOW ON THE BEAUTY OF NATURE IN A PRECISE MOMENT OF THE YEAR. ALL YEAR ROUND, BONSAI ARE TENDED SO AS TO BRING OUT

1 *Carpinus japonica* infructescence at the beginning of summer. 2-3 *Shari*, a dry wood formation on the trunk of a *Juniperus chinensis* var. *sargentii*. 4-5 A *Ginkgo biloba* leaf in its summer livery. 8 *Shohin*, a small *Corylopsis spicata* bonsai 18 cm (7 in) high. 11 *Prunus incisa*. 12-13 *Crataegus laevigata* 'Paul's Scarlet' flowers. 14 *Kokedama*, moss ball, with *Ginkgo biloba*. 15 *Kusamono*, a summer bonsai with herbaceous plants, grass and *Hosta*. A cool, refreshing and particularly graceful mini-landscape.

THEIR BEST FEATURES AT THE RIGHT MOMENT — IN WINTER WHEN THE FINE SUBTLE RAMIFICATIONS CAN BE ADMIRED IN THE LEAFLESS TREES ; IN SPRING WHEN THE FLOWERS OPEN AND LEAVES UNFURL ; IN SUMMER WHEN THE EXUBERANCE OF THE FOLIAGE HINTS AT THE ENORMOUS WORK UNDERWAY TO SUPPORT GROWTH AND IN AUTUMN, WITH THE RIPE FRUIT, CHANGING COLOUR OF THE LEAVES BEFORE THEY FALL AND MAJESTY OF THE CONIFERS.

IT IS NO ACCIDENT THAT THE BONSAI IN THE CRESPI BONSAI MUSEUM (ABOUT 200) ARE DISPLAYED IN ROTATION AT THE BEST MOMENT. THESE PAGES PRESENT THE MOST FASCINATING AND SURPRISING BONSAI, TRAINED BY THE MOST FAMOUS JAPANESE MASTERS, COLLECTED AND TENDED LOVINGLY BY THE MUSEUM'S FOUNDER, LUIGI CRESPI, DESCRIBED BY NOBUYUKI KAJIWARA, BONSAI MASTER AND MUSEUM DIRECTOR, SELECTED PERSONALLY BY SUSANNA CRESPI WHO HAS INHERITED THE PASSION FOR BONSAI TRANSMITTED BY HER FATHER, AND PHOTOGRAPHED BY FABIO PETRONI, MASTER OF STILL LIFE PHOTOGRAPHY, WHOSE LENS AND EYE AS SENSITIVE AS THAT OF A BIRD IN FLIGHT HAVE CAPTURED THE ASPECTS AND DETAILS WHICH MAKE EACH SPECIMEN UNIQUE.

ANNA MARIA BOTTICELLI

"Strength"

PINES ARE AN INTEGRAL PART OF THE WONDERFUL LANDSCAPE OF JAPAN. SYMBOL OF LONGEVITY AND CONSIDERED AS SPECIAL, THEY ARE ESSENTIAL ELEMENTS IN THE JAPANESE GARDEN. THE SAME IS TRUE OF THE JAPANESE ART OF BONSAI WHERE THE PINES REPRESENT THE EXTREME MINIATURISATION OF A NATURAL LANDSCAPE. TOGETHER WITH THE JUNIPER, FIR, LARCH, METASEQUOIA, YEW, CYPRESS AND TSUGA, PINES ARE CONIFERS, A VAST GROUP OF ARCHAIC PLANTS WHICH APPEARED ON THE EARTH IN THE CARBONIFEROUS PERIOD 300 MILLION YEARS AGO. ALMOST EXCLUSIVELY EVERGREEN, CONIFERS USUALLY GROW AS TREES (ALTHOUGH THERE ARE ALSO NUMEROUS BUSH FORMS, SUCH AS THE JUNIPER OR MUGO PINE) WITH LONG, POINTED MINIMAL NEEDLE- OR SCALE-LIKE LEAVES AND CONE-SHAPED WOODY FRUITS WITH HARD SCALES COMMONLY KNOWN AS PINE-CONES. TOUGH PLANTS WITH LEGENDARY LONGEVITY, LIGHT-LOVERS AND ABLE TO COLONISE COLD ARID ENVIRONMENTS, THEY FORM VAST FORESTS AT QUITE HIGH ALTITUDES, OR LIKE THE JUNIPER, GROW NEAR IMPERVIOUS WINDSWEPT COASTS, THEIR BRANCHES THRUSTING BRAVELY TOWARDS THE WAVES.

AUSTERE AND HARMONIOUS, CONIFERS ENTERED THE WORLD OF THE JAPANESE BONSAI IN THE MEJI PERIOD (1868-1912) AND SINCE THEN HAVE BEEN AMONG THE MOST IMPORTANT TREES IN ANY COLLECTION, INCLUDING THOSE BELONGING TO EUROPEAN AMATEURS. THE BEST LOVED SPECIES ARE THE CHINESE JUNIPER (*JUNIPERUS CHINENSIS*), THE JAPANESE BLACK PINE (*PINUS THUNBERGII*) AND THE JAPANESE WHITE PINE (*PINUS PENTAPHYLLA*).

NOBUYUKI KAJIWARA, *SENSEI* (BONSAI MASTER) AND CURATOR OF THE CRESPI BONSAI MUSEUM, HELPS US TO APPRECIATE THE BEAUTY OF THE CONIFER BONSAI DISPLAYED HERE, CENTURIES-OLD MASTERPIECES, SYMBOL OF TRADITIONAL CULTURE AND COMING FROM PRESTIGIOUS JAPANESE COLLECTIONS. HE EXPLAINS : "THE MOST STRIKING ASPECT OF THE CONIFER BONSAI IS THE MAJESTIC TRUNK. THE AGE IS NOT EXPRESSED SO MUCH BY THE ACTUAL SIZE OF THE BONSAI, AS BY WHAT WE CALL ITS "CONE-SHAPE," IN OTHER WORDS, THE DIFFERENCE IN DIAMETER FROM THE IMPOSING BASE TO THE SLENDER TAPERING APEX.

UNLIKE MAPLES WHICH HAVE A SMOOTH, VELVETY BARK, ONE OF THE ASPECTS CONTRIBUTING TO THE ANCIENT APPEARANCE OF CONIFER BONSAI IS THE APPEARANCE OF THE BARK WHICH IS ROUGH, THICK AND RETAINS ITS DISTINCTIVE CHARACTERISTICS RIGHT UP TO THE APEX."

PARTICULARLY APPRECIATED IN CONIFER BONSAI IS THE PRESENCE OF DEAD WOOD ON THE TRUNK, FORMED IN NATURE WHEN THE BARK DISINTEGRATES AND MAKING THE TREE SEEM OLDER. THE JAPANESE WORD FOR DEAD WOOD ON THE TRUNK IS *SHARI*, A REFERENCE TO THE REMAINS OF BUDDHA AND THE SAINTS. HERE IT RECOUNTS THE PAST LIFE OF THE TREE. FOR THE JAPANESE ONE OF THE BEST LOVED AND MOST FAMILIAR SPECIES, THE JUNIPER (*JUNIPERUS CHINENSIS*) MAKES A PARTICULARLY FASCINATING BASE ON WHICH TO CREATE THESE FORMATIONS. SPLENDID CURVES REMINISCENT OF DRAGONS' WINGS, OR INSUBSTANTIAL AS A DRESS BLOWING IN THE WIND, RESEMBLE BRANCHES BLEACHED BY THE SALT LADEN WIND THRUSTING OUT TOWARDS THE SEA.

BON SAI, THE LITERAL TRANSLATION OF THE IDEOGRAMS FORMING THE WORD BONSAI, MEANS "TREE PLANTED IN A POT." THIS CONFIRMS THE IMPORTANCE ATTACHED TO CHOOSING THE RIGHT POT IN WHICH TO GROW THE TREE. THE BEST CHOICE FOR CONIFERS IS AUSTERE UNGLAZED STONEWARE, LARGER WHEN THE LANDSCAPE PORTRAYS A WOOD, DEEPER WHEN THE TREE HAS A CASCADE FORM AND SUGGESTS THE VERTICAL DIMENSION OF THE MOUNTAIN.

IN CONSTANT TRANSFORMATION, THE PRECIOUS COLLECTION OF CONIFERS IN THE CRESPI BONSAI MUSEUM IS EXPANDED YEAR AFTER YEAR WITH PARTICULARLY FINE MASTERPIECES, SOME OF ENORMOUS VALUE, SUCH AS TWO *PINUS PENTAPHYLLA* (INCLUDING *PINUS PENTAPHYLLA* 'MIYAJIMA', APPRECIATED FOR THE BEAUTY OF ITS FOLIAGE AND RARITY), A YEW FROM MOUNT ISHIZUCHI COMING FROM ONE OF THE SEVEN SACRED PEAKS ON THE ISLAND OF SHIKOKU IN JAPAN AND A *JUNIPERUS CHINENSIS* 'ITOIGAWA'.

16-17 *Shari*, a dry wood formation on the trunk of a *Juniperus chinensis* var. *sargentii*.
18 A mountain *Suiseki*, stone modelled by nature with the power to evoke the natural landscape where the conifers live.

Chamaecyparis obtusa Sekka

Chamaecyparis obtusa is one of the most appreciated, if not the most common, of conifer bonsai. The rough bark on the trunk makes specimens even just a few years old seem ancient. The minute evergreen scale-like ovate leaves are dark green edged at the bottom with pale blue. The name Sekka ("petrified" in Japanese) refers to the very slow growth of this particular type of hinoki cypress. Its particular characteristic column or cone shape with layers in a fan arrangement makes this species particularly suitable for creating groups of trees on a "raft." The shallow oval stoneware container emphasises the landscape and helps the observer see the natural scenery portrayed by the trees clearly.

ENGLISH NAME **Hinoki cypress** ❊ ORIGIN **Japan** ❊ AGE **50 years**
❊ HEIGHT **60 cm (24 in)** ❊ HEIGHT IN NATURAL STATE **15-20 m (49-66 ft)**

Juniperus chinensis

The harmonious composition of plants on rock, *ishitsuki* in Japanese, enables the bonsai enthusiast to create enchanting landscapes, such as a crag, an island, a deep gorge, a waterfall or a rocky lake shore, just as it would be seen in nature. The evergreen conifer *Juniperus chinensis* lends itself particularly well to this technique which is highly creative as the resulting landscape is very appealing and simple to understand for those unfamiliar with the art of bonsai. This style requires greater attention to maintenance, particularly watering, as the roots of the juniper and accompanying small ferns and mosses adhere firmly to the rock, just as occurs on a cliff exposed to the sea. The composition is displayed in a *suiban*, a beige oval stoneware tray without drainage holes filled with water.

ENGLISH NAME **Chinese juniper**

ORIGIN **Japan**

AGE **50 years**

HEIGHT **70 cm (28 in)**

HEIGHT IN NATURAL STATE **20 m (66 ft)**

Juniperus chinensis
var. *sargentii*

Junipers collected in nature very often have dead parts at the ends of the trunk and some branches (the well-known *jin*) and these sometimes continue along the branches and trunk to form areas of dead wood known as *shari*. Particular ageing techniques can be used to recreate these extraordinary natural effects on juniper bonsai to accentuate the fascination of the specimen and make it more intensely evocative of the hostile severe environment where it normally grows. These parts, *jin* and *shari*, contribute much to the beauty of the bonsai and are the tangible signs of the effects of the austere climate and harshness of time. This informal upright specimen with sinuous trunk with impressive dead wood formations is topped by fine compact bright green foliage forming fascinating "cloud-like" layers. It has become one with the rectangular reddish brown stoneware pot with cut edges, decorative moulding and outward turned rim.

ENGLISH NAME **Juniper** ❊ ORIGIN **Japan** ❊ AGE **350 years** ❊ HEIGHT **105 cm (41 in)** ❊ HEIGHT IN NATURAL STATE **20 m (66 ft)**

Metasequoia glyptostroboides

Fossil findings suggest that the metasequoia already existed fifty million years ago. However, its discovery by chance in a Chinese forest dates back to 1941. Since then, thanks to the ease with which it can be grown from seed, the metasequoia has been cultivated throughout the world. The first seeds reaching Italy were germinated in the Borromeo botanical garden on Isola Madre in Lake Maggiore. Curiously, it is a deciduous conifer with leaves light green in spring, dark green in summer and turning red or golden yellow in the autumn before falling. The bonsai technique shows the light soft fern-like foliage of this naturally slender tree off to best advantage. The Crespi Bonsai Museum specimen with upright trunk growing in a rectangular stoneware pot with bevelled edges and outward turned rim was imported from the Japanese Musashino-en nursery in the 1990s as an unusual species.

ENGLISH NAME **Metasequoia** ❊ ORIGIN **Japan** ❊ AGE **60 years**
❊ HEIGHT **134 cm (53 in)** ❊ HEIGHT IN NATURAL STATE **up to 35 m (115 ft)**

Picea abies

ENGLISH NAME **Norway spruce**

✽

ORIGIN **Japan**

✽

AGE **80 years**

✽

HEIGHT **125 cm (49 in)**

✽

HEIGHT IN NATURAL STATE **35-55 m (115-180 ft)**

The Norway spruce is a conifer of north European origin, famous for its traditional use as a Christmas tree. It can be distinguished from other conifers by the square, rather than flat, cross-section of the needle-like leaves. It is one of the longest living species in the plant kingdom. Thanks to carbon dating, the University of Umeå in Sweden has established that a Norway spruce known as Old Tjikko is the oldest living tree in the world with 9,500 years. The evocative wood landscape, *yose-ue*, on a slab of stone in the Crespi Bonsai Museum is made up of trees with sinuous trunks in a harmonious arrangement – three individuals of the same species, but with different ages and dimensions. To achieve this high degree of harmony, precise rules of equilibrium and proportion have been respected.

Pinus pentaphylla

For many enthusiasts, long-lived evergreen pines are the first approach to the art of bonsai. During the first years of growth, they have a pyramid form. As they grow older, the plant's characteristic features are accentuated – crevices appear in the bark making it ever more interesting and the foliage becomes thicker and enhanced with splendid layers. *Pinus pentaphylla*, a native of Japan, can be recognised by the needle-like leaves in tufts of five elements (hence its name). The lightness of this double-trunk specimen derives from constant care of the leaves, together with application of copper wire on the branches to model the shape. The growth of pines is in fact closely linked to light which must always be abundant. Thinning of the tufts of needles is therefore fundamental to allow as much light as possible to penetrate to the inside of the plant. The specimen in the Crespi Bonsai Museum is grown in an exquisite rectangular brown stoneware Japanese *tokoname* pot with rim.

ENGLISH NAME **Japanese five-needle pine**

❖

ORIGIN **Japan**

❖

AGE **90 years**

❖

HEIGHT **110 cm (43 in)**

❖

HEIGHT IN NATURAL STATE **10-30 m (33-98 ft)**

Juniperus rigida

In its natural habitat in the north of China, Korea and Japan, the temple juniper is a large bush, sometimes a small tree, with irregular growth. The branches grow upwards and the twigs hang downwards bearing tufts of needle-like bright green leaves. In Japan it is typically grown in temple gardens, hence the name of temple juniper. In common with *Juniperus chinensis*, it is one of the species most commonly used in the art of bonsai and together they form a special group in collections and events, due both to the large number of specimens displayed and their distinctive beauty. In the specimen in the Crespi Bonsai Museum, trained in the formal upright style, the extraordinarily slender trunk supports ordered layers of branches and allows the light to penetrate and the air to circulate freely, communicating a great energy. The *tachiagari* (the bottom part of the trunk) transmits a great sense of strength, with the fine work performed on the white dead wood showing under the reddish brown bark.

ENGLISH NAME **Temple juniper** ❊ ORIGIN **Japan** ❊ AGE **100 years**
❊ HEIGHT **109 cm (43 in)** ❊ HEIGHT IN NATURAL STATE **8 m (26 ft)**

Pinus pentaphylla 'Miyajima'

The Miyajima Japanese five-needle pine is appreciated for the beauty of its foliage and its rarity. It grows on the island of Miyajima south of Hiroshima, famous for its floating tori marking the entrance to the Shinto sanctuary of Itsukushima-jinja and designated one of Japan's "three best panoramas." Originally belonging to the famous collection owned by Mr Morobayashi of Sedaka (prefecture of Fukuoka, Japan), the pine later became one of the rarest specimens in the Iwasaki private collection. It was transferred to the Crespi Bonsai Museum in March 2009 as a sign of esteem and appreciation of the work carried out by its founder, Luigi Crespi, in spreading the culture of the bonsai in Italy and Europe. The trunk and principal branches of this specimen are black pine, evident from the appearance of the bark on the trunk, while the elegant vegetation grafted on the branches is Miyajima Japanese five-needle pine. This particular process is known in Japanese as "change of dress." The tree with sinuous trunk grows in a rectangular brown stoneware pot with relief decoration, a fine reproduction of a famous ancient Chinese pot.

ENGLISH NAME **Miyajima Japanese five-needle pine**
✽
ORIGIN **Japan**
✽
AGE **450 years**
✽
HEIGHT **110 cm (43 in)**
✽
HEIGHT IN NATURAL STATE **Cultivated variety**

Pinus thunbergii

ENGLISH NAME **Japanese black pine**

❀

ORIGIN **Japan**

❀

AGE **100 years**

❀

HEIGHT **100 cm (39 in)**

❀

HEIGHT IN NATURAL STATE **15-20 m (49-66 ft)**

The Japanese black pine (*Pinus thunbergii*) is the most common conifer bonsai. Its distinctive features are the trunk with thick rough bark and long bright green needles, masculine traits compared to the airy elegant characteristics of the Japanese five-needle pine (*Pinus pentaphylla*). This specimen is striking for its imposing appearance and the conical shaped trunk with very wide base and very slender apex. The transition between these two parts is gradual and, in the case of the Japanese black pine, characterised by the roughness of the bark. In a bonsai, the difference between the diameter at the base of the trunk and that of the peripheral twigs is the real expression of its age. It is these characteristics, rather than just the 100 cm (39 in) height, which make this bonsai appear older than it actually is. And its years already amount to one hundred.

Juniperus chinensis var. *sargentii*

ENGLISH NAME **Juniper**

✻

ORIGIN **Japan**

✻

AGE **250 years**

✻

HEIGHT **100 cm (39 in)**

✻

HEIGHT IN NATURAL STATE **20 m (66 ft)**

The natural *sargentii* variety of the juniper (*Shinpaku*) is a prostrate open bush, native of the cool temperate zones of Japan and China and among the plants most frequently used in the art of bonsai. It is also especially common in Italy as, thanks to its adaptability to the most diverse environmental conditions, it responds well to all techniques. It is particularly suitable for dead wood techniques used to give the trees a highly evocative character. To avoid the bush looking artificial, nature must be taken as a model when setting out to "age" a juniper by forming *jin* imitating the effects of a lightning strike on the branches or working the dead wood on the trunk (*shari*). The result is a spectacular bleached formation on the trunk with the part of the bark left whole flaking as it matures.

ENGLISH NAME
Kometsuga

ORIGIN
Japan

AGE
95 years

HEIGHT
100 cm (39 in)

HEIGHT IN NATURAL STATE
10-13 m (33-43 ft)

Tsuga diversifolia

The Tsuga are evergreen conifers growing wild in the vast damp shady forests from the Himalayas to northern Burma and Japan and are also common in North America. *Tsuga diversifolia* comes from northern Japan where the climate is cool all year round. In the natural state, it grows as a bushy pyramid-shaped tree. The needle-like bright green leaves have two characteristic teeth at the apex. The specimen in the Crespi Bonsai Museum has a double trunk supporting orderly layers and shows the typical reddish brown bark which, with age, forms deep cracks and flakes in plaques.

Taxus cuspidata

A native of China and Japan, the Japanese yew is a slow-growing conifer reaching a height of 18 m (59 ft) in nature. It has a column-like growth habit, highly ramified and with compact vegetation. The attractive dark foliage consists of linear flat leaves with sharp points in an orderly arrangement. The majority of Japanese yews originate in the Hokkaido area of northern Japan and the same is also true of the yew bonsai masterpieces. Shaped by the Crespi Bonsai staff, this specimen has three trunks trained in a semi-cascade form and projecting beyond the pot. Particularly worthy of note is the imposing base giving this specimen stability and excellent balance between the main, second and third trunks.

ENGLISH NAME **Japanese yew** ✻ ORIGIN **Japan** ✻ AGE **75 years**
✻ LENGTH **50 cm (20 in)** ✻ HEIGHT IN NATURAL STATE **10-18 m (33-59 ft)**

"Elegance"

IN JAPAN, MAPLES ARE DEARLY LOVED FOR THE INNATE ELEGANCE OF THEIR APPEARANCE AND BECAUSE THEY SYMBOLISE THE GENTLENESS OF NATURE, GRACIOUS IN EVERY SEASON. THANKS TO THE CHARACTERISTIC REFINED CULTIVATION TECHNIQUES, THE ART OF THE BONSAI MANAGES TO EMPHASISE THE SOFT LIGHTNESS OF THE BRANCHES AND SILKY SMOOTHNESS OF THE BARK OF THESE TREES, SPECIAL PLANTS IN EVERY COLLECTION. TOGETHER WITH THE BEECH, HORNBEAM, LIQUIDAMBAR, STEWARTIA, SPINDLE AND GINKGO (MAINLY OF ORIENTAL ORIGIN), MAPLES BELONG TO THE ENORMOUS GROUP OF BROADLEAF TREES, OR RATHER, THE ANGIOSPERMS WHICH APPEARED ON EARTH DURING THE JURASSIC PERIOD ABOUT 135 MILLION YEARS AGO. THEY ARE MORE HIGHLY EVOLVED THAN CONIFERS, WITH FLOWERS ABLE TO ENSURE EFFECTIVE SEXUAL REPRODUCTION AND SEEDS ENCLOSED IN AN OVARY WHICH DEVELOPS INTO A FRUIT AFTER FERTILISATION.

IN THE JAPANESE TRADITIONAL CULTURE, BROADLEAF BONSAI ARE ALMOST EXCLUSIVELY DECIDUOUS SPECIES. ALTHOUGH THEY FLOWER AND PRODUCE FRUITS, THE MAIN POINTS OF INTEREST IN THIS CATEGORY OF BONSAI ARE THE LEAVES, THE DELICACY OF THE FIRST SHOOTS IN THE SPRING, THE VIVID GREEN OF THE LEAVES DURING THE SUMMER AND, FINALLY, THE BRIGHT COLOURS DURING AUTUMN. HOWEVER, WHETHER IN THE NATURAL STATE OR AS A BONSAI, THE FINEST FEATURE OF THESE TREES IS EVIDENT AFTER THE LEAVES HAVE FALLEN, REVEALING THE SILHOUETTE AND ELEGANT LIGHTNESS OF THE RAMIFICATIONS IN ALL THEIR MOST REFINED DETAILS. A WINDOW ON A RESTFUL LANDSCAPE WHICH COMMUNICATES CALM AND TRANQUILLITY. AS NOBUYUKI KAJIWARA, BONSAI MASTER AT THE CRESPI BONSAI MUSEUM, OBSERVING A MAPLE IN ITS WINTER LIVERY POINTS OUT : "A BIRD COULD FLY THROUGH ITS BRANCHES."

IN THE WESTERN CULTURE AND CHINA, ON THE OTHER HAND, BROADLEAF BONSAI ALSO INCLUDE EVERGREEN SPECIES WHICH KEEP THEIR LEAVES IN WINTER, RENEWING THEM PERIODICALLY BUT GRADUALLY, THUS MAINTAINING AN APPARENTLY UNCHANGING LIVERY. THESE FORM THE CATEGORY OF THE INDOOR BONSAI WHICH, UNLIKE ALL OTHER BONSAI AND WITH A FEW RARE EXCEPTIONS AND THE NECESSARY PRECAUTIONS AS REGARDS SUMMER, MUST BE GROWN INDOORS ALL YEAR ROUND. SUSANNA CRESPI, WHO LOVES ALL BONSAI, EXPLAINS : "THESE FAR FROM SUBTLE DIFFERENCES ARE EXPLAINED BY THE CHARACTERISTICS OF THE CLIMATE IN THE PLACES WHERE THE SPECIES GROW ORIGINALLY. THE FICUS, TEA TREE AND SNOWROSE, FOR EXAMPLE, COME FROM THE HOT AND TEMPERATE AREAS OF CHINA SO THE CORRESPONDING BONSAI

54-55 *Ginkgo biloba* leaves at the beginning of autumn. 56 *Kikkaseki*, natural stone with a chrysanthemum motif, symbol of immortality in the Japanese tradition. 57 *Kusamono*, summer bonsai with ornamental grasses.

MUST BE GROWN INDOORS ALL YEAR ROUND, JUST LIKE A HOUSEPLANT. ON THE OTHER HAND, DECIDUOUS BROADLEAF BONSAI COMING MAINLY FROM JAPAN ARE TYPICAL OF REGIONS WITH A COLD CLIMATE AND ARE THEREFORE GROWN OUTDOORS ALL YEAR ROUND, INCLUDING DURING THE WINTER."

THE CRESPI BONSAI MUSEUM HAS BOTH CATEGORIES : OUTDOOR OPEN-AIR BONSAI IN THE SPECIALLY DESIGNED STEEL AND CONCRETE STRUCTURE ; INDOOR BONSAI DISPLAYED IN THE NEIGHBOURING ELEGANT GLAZED PAGODA. THIS IS WHERE YOU CAN ADMIRE THE MOST IMPORTANT BONSAI : THE ANCIENT DECIDUOUS *GINKGO BILOBA*, THE FIRST BONSAI ACQUIRED BY LUIGI CRESPI MORE THAN 50 YEARS AGO AND THE INSPIRATION FOR HIS EXTRAORDINARY MUSEUM COLLECTION, AND THE CENTURIES-OLD EVERGREEN *FICUS RETUSA* AT THE CENTRE OF THE PAGODA UNDER A SPIRE, LOVINGLY TENDED BY THE ITALIAN EXPERTS IN THE CRESPI STAFF.

Acer buergerianum

SUMMER

ENGLISH NAME **Trident maple**

ORIGIN **Japan**

AGE **70 years**

HEIGHT **125 cm (49 in)**

HEIGHT IN NATURAL STATE **10 m (33 ft)**

A native of Asia, as are most of the known species, *Acer buergerianum* owes its Japanese name, *kaede* ("toad's hand") and English name, trident maple, to the particular shape of the leaf, divided into three well-defined pointed lobes. Common in the wild in eastern China and Taiwan, this deciduous tree with luxuriant foliage in summer and particularly attractive in autumn when the leaves change colour, has been one of the most sought-after subjects of the Japanese art of bonsai since ancient times. It is a robust long-lived species, easy to shape and responding well to cultivation techniques. The specimen on rock with exposed roots is particularly evocative during the winter when the perfection of its silhouette is displayed to full advantage. The sturdy roots (not trunks) with the bark flaking in places move sinuously along the rock and sink into the soil which nourishes them. The flared round brown stoneware pot with outward turned rim decorated with incisions and grooves gives particular impetus to this bonsai more than a metre tall.

Acer palmatum 'Deshojo'

In the art of bonsai, the 'Deshojo' variety of *Acer palmatum* (a typically Japanese species with the leaf divided into five well-defined lobes) is particularly appreciated for the constant spectacular transformations following the rhythm of the seasons – from the moment of the tender spring shoots, through the luxuriant summer foliage to the magnificent colour of the leaves in autumn. It is no less interesting after it sheds its leaves to reveal an elegant silhouette and fine unmistakable ramifications. Easy to shape, it responds well to cultivation techniques. All its best characteristics are accentuated by the *kabaduchi* multiple trunk style, obtained when a number of trunks (usually an odd number) are allowed to develop from the shoots formed on a single root. The final effect is of a group of trees sharing a single root.

This variety of Japanese maple (*Acer palmatum*) has two distinctive characteristics. The first is the bark which, instead of being smooth and silvery like the typical species, is dark with deep crevices (*arakawa* in Japanese). This is the result of a natural mutation which can be induced in other specimens only through sophisticated reproduction techniques using grafting, cuttings or marcottage. The second is the unusual "raft" style (*ikadabuki* in Japanese) representing a fallen tree with the side branches converted into trees. This creates the image of a group of individual plants growing from a horizontal trunk. The perspective effect is quite original and enhances the fascination of the specimen in all seasons, just as occurs in nature where the phenomenon is very frequent. The specimen is growing in a light blue glazed oval rimmed pot.

SUMMER

Acer palmatum

ENGLISH NAME **Japanese maple** ❋ ORIGIN **Japan** ❋ AGE **80 years**
❋ HEIGHT **92 cm (36 in)** ❋ HEIGHT IN NATURAL STATE **6-10 m (20-33 ft)**

AUTUMN

The Japanese maple (*Acer palmatum*) is a deciduous species, in other words, it sheds its leaves in the autumn, then renews them in spring. It grows slowly in the form of a bush or small tree and can be recognised by the light rounded foliage, seven-lobed palmate leaves and light coloured bark. Forefather of numerous varieties, such as 'Deshojo' with red leaves, the minute 'Kiyohime' and 'Shishigashira' with apple-green curly leaves, it is one of the most appreciated species in the art of bonsai as it is robust, easy to shape and responds well to pinching and pruning techniques. During the winter after the leaves have been shed, the full fascination of this specimen in informal upright style is revealed, with its elegant silhouette and fine ramifications.

Acer palmatum
Arakawa

ENGLISH NAME **Japanese maple *arakawa***

❁

ORIGIN **Japan**

❁

AGE **110 years**

❁

HEIGHT **90 cm (35 in)**

❁

HEIGHT IN NATURAL STATE **not indicated as this is a natural mutation**

SUMMER

AUTUMN

Whatever the season, the most eye-catching aspect of this *Acer palmatum* to the Western observer is the bark with its deep clearly-defined crevices. A natural mutation, this characteristic is known as *arakawa* meaning rough bark in Japanese. To the eyes of an Oriental observer on the other hand, the most striking aspects are its majestic appearance and the shape of the base of the trunk which show that this bonsai is well rooted in the soil and how much attention the *sensei* (master) has devoted to working the *nebari* (trunk base). Despite its age (more than 100 years), there is still an extraordinary lightness to the movement of the branches of this bonsai, so well defined, fine and never rigid. Another delightful feature is the internodes (the distance between the nodes) which are very short and numerous. This leads naturally to the formation of dense ramifications with small leaves. In autumn, the leaves turn from their summer green through yellow to a bright, warm golden red. This specimen in informal upright style with sinuous trunk is growing in a light blue glazed oval rimless pot.

Acer palmatum 'Kotohime'

SPRING

ENGLISH NAME **Japanese maple 'Kotohime'**
✳
ORIGIN **Japan**
✳
AGE **70 years**
✳
HEIGHT **85 cm (33 in)**
✳
HEIGHT IN NATURAL STATE **5-6 m (16-20 ft)**

SUMMER

Among the cultivars of the Japanese maple *Acer palmatum*, 'Kotohime' (meaning small harp) is the smallest and most graceful, the first to open its buds at the end of winter and clothe itself in new leaves, naturally minute, deeply divided into lobes and arranged in tufts along the branches. Their pale green colour barely glimpsed beneath the pink, orange and red nuances along the edges is particularly enchanting. In summer, it is a triumph of green with bluish lights, turning to yellow and orange again in autumn. Growing in a pale blue glazed oval rimmed pot, the specimen in the Crespi Bonsai Museum is in double trunk style and grows from a single root. One of the trunks slants slightly towards the front, emphasising the perspective effect and making the plant seem deeper. In turn, the arrangement of the branches and the vegetation give the effect of a single tree.

Carpinus japonica

ENGLISH NAME **Japanese hornbeam**

✻

ORIGIN **Japan**

✻

AGE **40-70 years**

✻

HEIGHT **90 cm (35 in)**

✻

HEIGHT IN NATURAL STATE **4-8 m (13-26 ft)**

AUTUMN

The Japanese hornbeam (*Carpinus japonica*) is appreciated for the lightness of its foliage which is renewed every year in the spring. Easy to train as a bonsai, it has an elegant but natural growth, thanks to the grey bark with darker furrows and streaks. It is an elegant deciduous tree with voluminous foliage, fine ramifications and separate male and female inflorescences in spring. The female flowers go on to form fruits in the summer. Both edges of the simple bright green leaves with raised veins are toothed. In autumn they turn golden and reddish, then brown. The woodland style, *yose-ue*, of this bonsai transmits the charming effect of a corner of nature through the harmonious arrangement of a number of plants of the same species but with different ages and sizes in a single container. The irregular spacing between the trunks and contrasting diameters and heights of the specimens, with the thin trunks in the background and towards the edges, help accentuate the perspective effect, creating the appearance of dense vegetation admired from afar. The specimen grows in a brown oval stoneware pot with external rim.

WINTER

AUTUMN

Euonymus alatus

Widespread in Japan and central China, this deciduous bush attracts the attention of bonsai enthusiasts for the spectacular foliage turning crimson in autumn. The fruits which form after fertilisation of the minute flowers in the spring and begin to ripen with the first cold are also pale red and topped by a curious dark four-lobed capsule. Equally distinctive are the flat lateral appendages which emerge from the youngest branches to then become permanent. These unique structures develop from the change of bark which is deposited along longitudinal cracks. The appendages resemble small wings, earning the plant its scientific species name of *alatus*. The bonsai is trained in an informal upright style.

ENGLISH NAME **Winged spindle**

❖

ORIGIN **Japan**

❖

AGE **65 years**

❖

HEIGHT **80 cm (31 in)**

❖

HEIGHT IN NATURAL STATE **2.5 m (8 ft)**

SPRING

AUTUMN

Fagus crenata

The beech is greatly appreciated by bonsai enthusiasts for the splendid colour variations of its foliage, making it interesting at any time of year. In common with its European counterpart (*Fagus sylvatica*), the root system of the Japanese beech (*Fagus crenata*) is well adapted to life in a pot, a special gift invaluable to a plant destined for training as a bonsai. Grown as a solitary specimen in a formal upright style, it is freed from the numerous ramifications to take on a slender aspect with well-spaced layers and ramifications becoming ever finer towards the apex. The work of the *sensei* (master) is more evident during the winter after the leaves have been shed, when the structure of the tree stands out in its full beauty and you can best admire the bark with its distinctive silvery grey colour, smooth in even the oldest specimens. The longer hours of light bring out the new leaves marked by evident veins, pale green in the spring, bright green during the summer and golden brown in autumn.

ENGLISH NAME **Japanese beech**

ORIGIN **Japan**

AGE **90 years**

HEIGHT **110 cm (43 in)**

HEIGHT IN NATURAL STATE **35 m (115 ft)**

WINTER

SPRING

Fagus sylvatica

ENGLISH NAME **European beech**

❖

ORIGIN **Italy**

❖

AGE **100 years**

❖

HEIGHT **100 cm (39 in)**

❖

HEIGHT IN NATURAL STATE **30 m (98 ft)**

A species with a familiar appearance, *Fagus sylvatica* is a deciduous tree native to Europe, very common in England in woods in the natural state and in public parks and private gardens. It has a trunk with elegant form and colour and produces foliage which, although exuberant, is easy to contain when grown as a bonsai through autumn and spring pruning of the branches and twigs to obtain the required silhouette. The oval glossy leaves with slightly wavy edge, light green when young, turning yellow then purple red in the autumn before falling, regrow each spring, emerging from the tapering pointed buds which form on the branches during the previous summer. This slanting style bonsai trained in Italy has an imposing trunk base. It is here in the oldest part, in harmony with the foliage, that the tree expresses its full force in clinging to the ground, just as occurs in a natural landscape. The specimen with its sinuous trunk is growing in a rimless speckled green glazed pot.

Ginkgo biloba

WINTER

SUMMER

AUTUMN

ENGLISH NAME **Ginkgo**

❊

ORIGIN **Japan**

❊

AGE **140 years**

❊

HEIGHT **80 cm (31 in)**

❊

HEIGHT IN NATURAL STATE **up to 30 m (98 ft)**

A *Ginkgo biloba* bonsai is beautiful in all seasons – in winter, when only the essential silhouette of the trunk is visible with its dark grey grooved and furrowed bark communicating great strength; in spring when the tender green leaves on the naked grey branches start to unfurl to the sun; in summer when it proudly wears its dense foliage and in autumn when the leaves turn to a dazzling golden yellow colour before falling. The globe-shaped fruits, first greenish and then yellow when ripe, appear on the plants bearing female flowers. The species name, *biloba*, perfectly describes the morphology of the flat fan-shaped leaves with their radial pattern of nerves partially incised in the centre. It appeared on the Earth long before the conifers in the Mesozoic period and is a primordial species, the only member of the *Ginkgoaceae* family, probably of Chinese origin. In Japan where it is traditionally considered as sacred, the ginkgo is often grown near Buddhist temples. This ancient specimen in formal upright style was the first bonsai acquired by Luigi Crespi more than 50 years ago and the first plant which inspired his extraordinary museum collection.

Liquidambar formosana

SUMMER

AUTUMN

ENGLISH NAME **Formosan gum**

ORIGIN **Japan**

AGE **85 years**

HEIGHT **123 cm (48 in)**

HEIGHT IN NATURAL STATE **18-20 m (59-66 ft)**

A large tree with thick bark common growing wild in the temperate zones of southern China and Taiwan, the *Liquidambar formosana* can be easily distinguished from the American species, *Liquidambar styraciflua* (easier to cultivate in our climate) by the leaves with their three, rather than five, lobes. Although the Chinese species is still rare in bonsai collections, it attracts great interest among enthusiasts for its leaves, emerald green in spring and summer, then turning to yellow, sometimes red, at the end of autumn before falling. This bonsai in informal upright style features an imposing *tachiagari*, the bottom part of the trunk up to the first branch. The entire sinuous trunk with rough bark provides an effective contrast to the fine ramifications and softness of the foliage.

Stewartia monadelpha

AUTUMN

WINTER

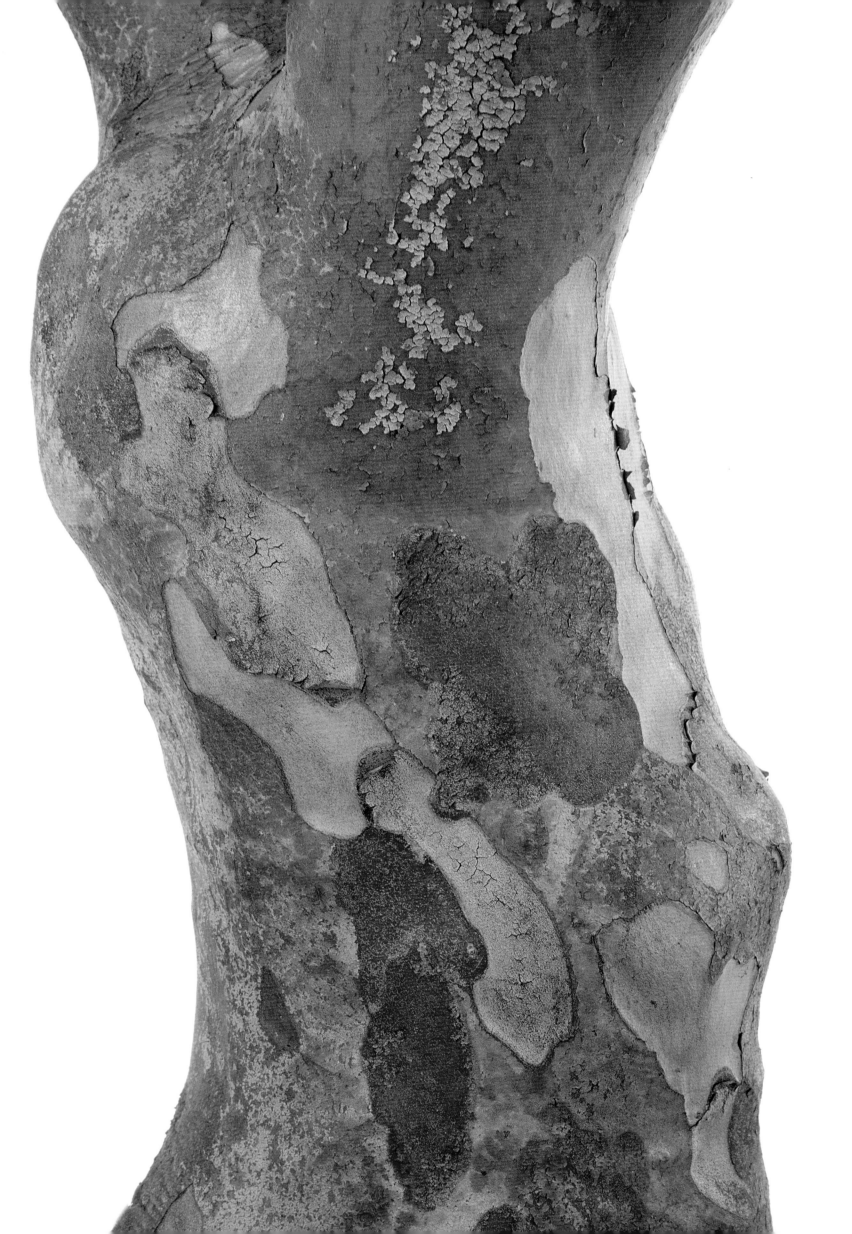

SPRING

There are few species with characteristics as easy to reproduce in a pot as the *Stewartia monadelpha*. Bonsai enthusiasts are well aware of this and when recreating a landscape, usually take their inspiration from plants growing in nature. A large tree growing wild in Japan, this species in the *Theaceae* family (the same as the *Camellia* genus) is appreciated for the distinctive appearance of the cinnamon red bark which flakes in strips leaving distinct marks on the trunk and the leaves, opaque green in spring and summer and with red and orange nuances in autumn before falling. The summer blossoming is very elegant, thanks to the simple white fragrant flowers with saffron yellow stamens, resembling those of the camellia. The specimen in informal upright style with sinuous trunk is growing in a green glazed rectangular pot with cut edges and outward turned rim.

ENGLISH NAME **Stewartia** ❊ ORIGIN **Japan** ❊ AGE **95 years** ❊ HEIGHT **105 cm (41 in)** ❊ HEIGHT IN NATURAL STATE **20 m (66 ft)**

Ficus retusa

ENGLISH NAME **Cuban laurel**

✿

ORIGIN **China**

✿

AGE **50 years**

✿

HEIGHT **55 cm (22 in)**

✿

HEIGHT IN NATURAL STATE **10 m (33 ft)**

This most classical of indoor bonsai belongs to a species of tree in the
Moraceae family which includes all the *Ficus* species found throughout
the warm-temperate areas of south-east Asia. This semi-cascade
specimen is truly fascinating, shaped to interpret the modern taste in
bonsai – an imposing and skilfully woven *nebari* (root base), emphasising
the slanting trunk with beige bark supporting a number of well-defined
layers of vegetation. Thanks to its perfect proportions, the details of
the shaping can best be admired from close up. The dark blue glazed
pot with decisive lines has also been chosen to be observed from
close up. Its feet physically raise the bonsai, allowing the foliage to
fall elegantly down beyond the edge.

Ficus formosanum

There are about 600 species in the *Ficus* genus, mostly coming from hot tropical and subtropical regions, such as the island of Formosa crossed by the Tropic of Cancer. At our latitude, the evergreen *Ficus formosanum* is therefore an indoor species. It loves the warmth of the house and, thanks to the texture of the lymph and liquid rich leaves, tolerates low air humidity well. This specimen with smooth grey bark modelled by the Crespi Bonsai staff attracts attention for its double-trunk style and well-spaced layers with leaves distributed with great lightness. But its finest feature is the delightful web of aerial roots growing out of the branches and reaching downwards to bury themselves in the soil, thickening over time to form evocative "pillars" supporting the fronds. The outer branches can thus extend with great balance beyond the profile of the pot.

ENGLISH NAME **Formosan ficus**

❊

ORIGIN **China**

❊

AGE **80 years**

❊

LENGTH **54 cm (21 in)**

❊

HEIGHT IN NATURAL STATE **20 m (66 ft)**

ENGLISH NAME **Kusamaki**

ORIGIN **Japan**

AGE **75 years**

HEIGHT **90 cm (35 in)**

HEIGHT IN NATURAL STATE **20 m (66 ft)**

Podocarpus macrophyllus

Common in Japan, China and Vietnam, the kusamaki is a slow-growing evergreen conifer with vivid dark green leathery lanceolate leaves arranged in dense spirals which give off a fresh fragrance when rubbed. The interesting bark flakes irregularly. This specimen in informal upright style with sinuous trunk shaped by the Crespi staff grows in a striped green glazed oval pot. The beauty of the *nebari* (root base) which merges with the design of the first part of the trunk, *tachiagari*, and the arrangement of the branches in well-spaced layers make this a valuable specimen with an unmistakeable structure. During the hottest months of the year, it can be growth outdoors in bright shade. In the winter, on the other hand, it is best protected from the cold. It is an excellent indoor species.

Sageretia theezans

The genus *Sageretia*, native to central and southern Asia and the milder regions of North America, includes a dozen or so species of evergreen bush with slender rigid branches, a characteristic bark flaking in plaques and oval slightly toothed leaves. Small white flowers appear in summer, followed by dark blue berries. *Sageretia theezans* grows wild in the south of China and its natural habitat is characterised by a hot climate. In cooler temperate regions it is therefore grown as an indoor bonsai. Its balanced orderly growth makes it one of the most suitable varieties for growing as a bonsai. It tolerates pruning well and therefore offers great satisfaction to bonsai growers who love pruning, creating and maintaining the plant in a specific shape, such as this cascade form. The dimensions of the dark blue glazed pot with relief decorations show the growth habit of this hundred-year old tree off to the full, with its foliage falling freely over the edge.

ENGLISH NAME **Chinese sweet plum** ✳ ORIGIN **China** ✳ AGE **95 years** ✳ HEIGHT **57 cm (22 in)** ✳ HEIGHT IN NATURAL STATE **3 m (10 ft)**

Murraya paniculata

The impetus of the informal upright style of this ancient *Murraya paniculata* bonsai more than a metre tall is emphasised by the particular way in which the dead wood, *shari*, on a portion of the trunk has been worked. Stripped of bark this is bleached by the sunlight, the same effect as caused in nature when a tree is struck by lightning. The combination of elegant delicate leaves and light coloured smooth trunk with a natural silky appearance makes the *Murraya paniculata* highly appreciated in China and India where it grows wild. As it is a tropical species, in regions with a temperate climate, it is grown exclusively as an indoor bonsai. It is attractive in all seasons, but particularly evocative when it flowers. For their shape and fragrance, the white bell-shaped flowers resemble those of the jasmine, while the small brightly coloured berries which form in summer resemble miniature oranges.

ENGLISH NAME **Orange jessamine** ❋ ORIGIN **China** ❋ AGE **200 years**
❋ HEIGHT **120 cm (47 in)** ❋ HEIGHT IN NATURAL STATE **3 m (10 ft)**

Ulmus parvifolia

The Chinese elm has a long history of pot cultivation. Among the species grown as bonsai, this is the most resistant and adaptable to all types of climate. As it is a native of the tropical and sub-tropical zones of China, during the winter it must be protected from the cold weather and cultivated indoors. In the summer, on the other hand, to keep it healthy and compact it must be kept outside in full sun, protected from direct sunlight only during the hottest months. The most fascinating characteristic of this elm trained in a semi-cascade form is the contrast between the majestic appearance and the delicate peripheral ramifications which grow thinner at the apex of the bonsai. This result can be obtained only through constant care and meticulous selective pruning of the branches and pinching of the tender shoots. The handmade pot painted with the Great Wall of China shows off the majesty of the trunk to full advantage and leaves the foliage free to project beyond the edge.

ENGLISH NAME **Chinese elm** ❖ ORIGIN **Taiwan** ❖ AGE **130 years** ❖ LENGTH **140 cm (55 in)** ❖ HEIGHT IN NATURAL STATE **20 m (66 ft)**

Ficus retusa

ENGLISH NAME **Cuban laurel**

❋

ORIGIN **China**

❋

AGE **1000 years**

❋

HEIGHT **290 cm (114 in)**

❋

HEIGHT IN NATURAL STATE **10 m (33 ft)**

This is the most important tree, the flagship of the Crespi collection. This unique centuries-old tree arrived in Italy in 1986 from China after negotiations lasting more than ten years. Winner of numerous awards at international events, its value is inestimable. Its origins are lost in the memory of generations of expert bonsai growers and thanks to centuries of care with the most appropriate techniques, it has achieved matchless perfection and harmony. The spectacular trunk consisting of a dense network of aerial roots grows in an unusual pot made and fired in a single block, the world's largest bonsai pot. The daily care lavished on a bonsai so old and unusual requires great experience and a refined sensitivity to satisfy the tree's needs for the right moisture and temperature in all seasons. The great harmony of its form is the result of a gradual process of adaptation to the environment and its maturity is emphasised by that special patina only a masterpiece can emanate. Its strong personality moves the visitor entering the glass pagoda where it is housed in the Crespi Bonsai Museum where it never fails to arouse great respect for its long existence and mysterious history.

"Surprise"

Nobuyuki Kajiwara, bonsai master of the Crespi Bonsai Museum, points out that in the eyes of the Westerner, the emotions of watching a bud open is accompanied by surprise to note that the flowers appear almost out of proportion with respect to the slender dimensions of the branches on which they grow. And in fact, while the roots, trunks and leaves of the bonsai may be miniaturised, the flowers are the same size as the original species. And the same is true when the fruits appear.

At the Crespi Bonsai Museum, the flowering period is extraordinarily long and inviting as the trees on display belong to very different species. The first to appear are the golden yellow (the most luminous colour after white) flowers which open up on the wintersweet and certain jasmines, followed by the white flowers of the Japanese apricot, *Prunus mume*, the earliest *Prunus species* and one of the best loved. This is followed immediately by a succession of camellias, cornelians, hazels and magnolias. Various species of *Prunus* return with all their charm, including ornamental flowering species such as *Prunus x kanzakura* and the flowering plum (*Prunus domestica*), together with fruiting species such as the cherry (*Prunus avium*). April brings the Chinese roses (such as the Banks' rose) into flower, along with other species in the *Rosaceae* family such as spirea, hawthorn and flowering quince. May is the month of the azaleas and it is no coincidence that in Japan, cultivars of *Rhododendron indicum* (the species from which all azaleas derive) are known as *satsuki* meaning the fifth month (which is, of course, May). Then it is the turn of the wisteria. In a number of species which bloom in the spring or summer, the flowers are followed by ripening of the fruits and these, together with the changing livery of the leaves, bring new colour at the beginning of autumn. To give these extraordinary spectacles, the trees must work hard during spring and summer when the photosynthesis of the leaves provides them with abundant resources. In the case of flowering and fruiting bonsai, great attention is again paid to choosing the pots which are often glazed and in colours contrasting with those of the flowers.

150-151 *Wisteria japonica*, Japanese wisteria, in the spring.   152 *Suiseki*, small stone modelled by nature conjuring up images of spring cherry blossom.
153 *Kusamono*, summer bonsai of ornamental herbaceous plants in a handmade pot.

Chaenomeles speciosa 'Toyo-Nishiki'

With 'Toyo-Nishiki', a particular flowering quince cultivar created in Japan, it is the colour differences of the blossoms which immediately strike the eye. Red, pink or pinkish and white petals can be found on the same branch, not even on different branches. And it is not rare to see variations in the colours of the petals belonging to the same flower. This specimen with multiple trunk (*kabudachi*), growing from the selection of an uneven number of shoots developing from a single root, is a hundred years old and expresses its full history with great harmony. The bonsai master's constant care of the tree transmits a great sense of energy. Flowering begins during the first week of spring and proceeds gradually, bud after bud, followed by development of the first small leaves. The green glazed pot with decorative relief moulding portraying floral motifs and light feet enhances the characteristics of the tree.

ENGLISH NAME **Flowering quince**
ORIGIN **Japan** AGE **100 years**
HEIGHT **70 cm (28 in)** HEIGHT IN NATURAL STATE **2-3 m (7-10 ft)**

Chaenomeles speciosa

ENGLISH NAME **Flowering quince**

✽

ORIGIN **Japan**

✽

AGE **50 years**

✽

HEIGHT **40 cm (16 in)**

✽

HEIGHT IN NATURAL STATE **2 m (7 ft)**

Among bonsai enthusiasts, the flowering quince is one of the most representative species. A member of the same family as the rose (*Rosaceae*), it is a spiny compact deciduous or semi-evergreen bush with rough bark. The ease with which it branches is emphasised by repeated pruning, encouraging the production of short twigs. In this specimen, the work of the *sensei* (master) has made imposing roots emerge above the soil, giving the bonsai an austere appearance, softened at the end of winter by a profusion of bright orange-red flowers, as large as in nature – 2.5 cm (1 in) in diameter. The length of flowering is legendary and it is not rare for it to continue until the appearance of the first medium-green coloured leaves. It is grown in the sun and watered regularly to guarantee the right alternation of dry and wet substrate.

WINTER

Malus himekokoh

ENGLISH NAME **Japanese crab apple**

❋

ORIGIN **Japan**

❋

AGE **80 years**

❋

HEIGHT **110 cm (43 in)**

❋

HEIGHT IN NATURAL STATE **5-6 m (16-20 ft)**

The small 5-6 diameter apples which ripen in the autumn on the *Malus himekokoh* bonsai, an all-Japanese species (one of the most attractive and also appreciated for its delicate spring blossoms) are said to be tasty as well as a delight to see. Its remarkable height emphasises the slant of the trunk, imposing at the base and gradually tapering towards the apex. Stronger and more numerous on one side, the branches are visually balanced by the fine twigs the bonsai master has chosen to retain on the opposite side. On the left, the trunk has been worked to expose the light coloured dead wood, standing out between the folds of old grey bark. To obtain more flower buds and subsequently fruits, the tree requires pruning in August. Similarly, to avoid fatiguing the plant, the fruits should ideally be thinned as soon as ripening begins, leaving just one to three on each twig.

Citrus x *myrtifolia*

It stands out from other citrus trees for the absence of thorns and small, leathery pointed leaves resembling those of the myrtle, hence the botanical name *Citrus* x *myrtifolia*. Most probably it is not therefore a pure species, but a mutation of the Seville orange. In its natural state, it is a medium to small plant with a bushy growth habit and short compact ramifications. It produces a large quantity of bitter tasting fruits with fragrant peel which decorate the branches for a number of months. Together with its slow growth, these characteristics make the myrtle-leaved orange particularly appreciated by bonsai growers, including beginners. The specimen in the Crespi Bonsai Museum is a graceful informal upright tree, very different from the natural bush, made to seem older than its actual age by the work of the bonsai master.

ENGLISH NAME **Myrtle-leaved orange tree** ❈ ORIGIN **Indonesia**
❈ AGE **45 years** ❈ HEIGHT **58 cm (23 in)**
❈ HEIGHT IN NATURAL STATE **3 m (10 ft) at most**

WINTER

Punica granatum 'Nejikan'

AUTUMN

SUMMER

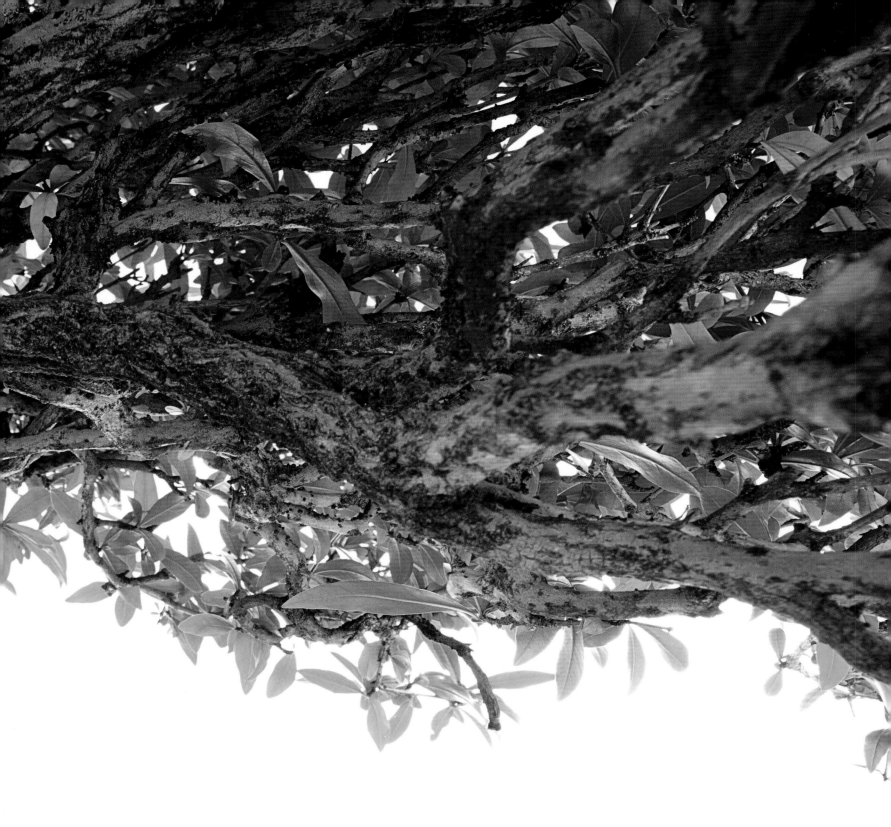

Apple with numerous seeds... this is the meaning of the name pomegranate, a small tree quite common in the Mediterranean basin with the peculiarity of retaining the ripe fruits even during the winter. The cold splits open the leathery casing of the fruit, exposing the small juicy ruby red seeds. With its large red flowers in spring and fruit slightly smaller than the typical species, the pomegranate cultivar most commonly grown by Japanese bonsai enthusiasts is "Nejikan," appreciated for its bark which naturally tends to twist and curl in an anticlockwise direction as the tree grows. During the summer, the dense foliage of small green leaves allows the gaze to appreciate the full beauty of the *tachiagari* (the first part of the trunk from the base to the first branch) which merges perfectly with the *nebari*, the swollen base of the roots which anchor the tree to the soil. When the leaves are shed in winter, the dense fine ramifications are striking. It is not hard to imagine its silhouette standing out against the background of a limpid blue sky.

ENGLISH NAME **Pomegranate** ✳ ORIGIN **Japan** ✳ AGE **80 years** ✳ HEIGHT **95 cm (37 in)** ✳ HEIGHT IN NATURAL STATE **2-4 m (7-13 ft)**

WINTER

Elaeagnus pungens

ENGLISH NAME **Silverthorn**

❀

ORIGIN **Japan**

❀

AGE **55 years**

❀

HEIGHT **95 cm (37 in)**

❀

HEIGHT IN NATURAL STATE **4-5 m (13-16 ft)**

A native of China and Japan, in the natural state the silverthorn is a dense thorny bush with an impenetrable mass of evergreen leaves. Quite easy to train, the bonsai form is relieved of the numerous ramifications and assumes the appearance of a small tapering tree with well-spaced layers. The growing technique involves drastic pruning of the old branches during the winter and pinching of the young branches during the summer. The constant work makes the apexes slenderer and gives the specimen an appearance of lightness. Of the numerous leathery dark green leaves with wavy edge supported on a short petiole, almost exclusively those on the upper side of the branches are left to improve visibility of the small pinkish hanging fruits. Resembling small olives, they begin to form in the winter and ripen in the spring.

Pseudocydonia sinensis

AUTUMN

This small tree of Chinese origin, a member of the *Rosaceae* family, has been grown as a bonsai in Japan since time immemorial for a number of interesting reasons. In spring it is covered in pink blossom, then in the summer, the fruits start to ripen as soon as the plant is covered by a voluminous bright green mantle of medium-large leaves. At first measuring just a few centimetres, in autumn when the leaves take on the typical bronze and red nuances, the Chinese quinces swell and grow to considerable dimensions (sometimes even exceeding 10 cm [4 in] long), becoming a vivid golden yellow and giving off an intense fragrance. To avoid weakening the plant, only a very few fruits should be left to ripen. The distinctive bark on the trunk flakes in plaques, exposing the dark wood underneath and giving a dappled appearance. The combination with an ivory coloured pot is particularly interesting, emphasising the colour of the fruit and foliage in its autumn livery.

SPRING

ENGLISH NAME **Chinese quince** ❈ ORIGIN **Japan** ❈ AGE **70 years** ❈ HEIGHT **103 cm (41 in)** ❈ HEIGHT IN NATURAL STATE **6 m (20 ft)**

SUMMER

SPRING

Crataegus laevigata 'Paul's Scarlet'

In the countryside in May, the decisive change in season is marked by blooming of the hawthorn, a thorny deciduous bush producing a spectacular profusion of bunches of white flowers in spring. The most striking feature of 'Paul's Scarlet,' a cultivar of the typical species, is the small delicate red double-corolla flowers resembling miniature roses. And it could hardly be otherwise, given that the rose and hawthorn both belong to the same family, the *Rosaceae*. The plant's vigour is emphasised in this bonsai, a masterpiece with its informal upright growth and dense horizontal branches creating layers lightened by the slender growing tips. The new distinctive three-lobed leaves appear as spring awakes. The bright green glazed rimless pot shows off the delicacy of the foliage to full effect.

ENGLISH NAME **English hawthorn 'Paul's Scarlet'** ❖ ORIGIN **Japan** ❖ AGE **80 years** ❖ HEIGHT **103 cm (41 in)** ❖ HEIGHT IN NATURAL STATE **4-8 m (13-26 ft)**

SPRING

Rhododendron indicum 'Kakuo'

In Japan, the azalea symbolises spring and is one of the trees most frequently used to create bonsai, together with maples and pines. It has all the ideal characteristics for this refined art. As well as flowering regularly in May, it has minute leaves, an attractive trunk, a good *nebari* (trunk base) and above all, fast growth. It is not difficult to make it flower and this is the objective of the care lavished throughout the year. However, it is curiously easier to make a young specimen flower than an already shaped tree in which even the points where the flowers will appear are chosen in advance. The evergreen 'Kakuo', a cultivar with flowers tinged with various intensities of pink, can be appreciated all year round. It is particularly suitable for training in a layered style. The design of the trunk and distribution of the imposing branches make this specimen particularly valuable.

ENGLISH NAME **Azalea**

❁

ORIGIN **Japan**

❁

AGE **95 years**

❁

HEIGHT **78 cm (31 in)**

❁

HEIGHT IN NATURAL STATE **2 m (7 ft)**

AUTUMN

Camellia sasanqua

A close relative of the tea plant (*Camellia sinensis*), the Yuletide camellia is one of the most highly appreciated flowers in Japan, thanks to its seductive simplicity and enchanting blooms which open as soon as the first cold weather arrives as though to attenuate the grey of the long winter. A native of the Japanese island of Okinawa where it is known as "sazanka" (meaning mountain tea flower), it is a long-lived erect tree with a compact appearance. The example in the Crespi Bonsai Museum is rare for its height, almost a metre. The thick trunk evoking a landscape in close-up has grey smooth bark concealing the hard wood. It has dense harmonious foliage, a perfect cone shape made up of branches with short internodes and leathery evergreen leaves, shiny dark green on the top and opaque light green beneath. Thanks to the skilful summer pruning and thinning of the numerous buds in the autumn, the bright pink petals open with great harmony and grace on the youngest leaves.

ENGLISH NAME **Yuletide camellia** ❋ ORIGIN **Japan**
❋ AGE **60 years** ❋ HEIGHT **93 cm (37 in)**
❋ HEIGHT IN NATURAL STATE **2 m (7 ft)**

Rhododendron indicum 'Kinsai'

Everything in 'Kinsai' expresses a unique strength combined with lightness. The strength derives from a *tachiagari* (the part from the bottom of the trunk to the first branch) exceptionally formed by the patient work of the bonsai masters who have trained it for about a century. The sense of lightness is communicated by the balanced position of the layers bearing a myriad of ever finer branches and by the minute leaves. In this fine cultivar of *Rhododendron indicum*, a bush originating in the Himalayan regions of Asia and the Japanese mountains, particular attention has been paid to the moment of flowering, the most striking aspect during May when the petals open up, distracting attention from the form of the bonsai. Here, 'Kinsai' was deliberately photographed with very few flowers open in order to better appreciate the marvellous shape and perfect layers with the flower buds all facing upwards.

ENGLISH NAME **Azalea**

❈

ORIGIN **Japan**

❈

AGE **120 years**

❈

HEIGHT **91 cm (36 in)**

❈

HEIGHT IN NATURAL STATE **2 m (7 ft)**

SPRING

Prunus x *kanzakura*

In Japan, the occasion of the spring cherry blossom, *hana-mi*, is a national event accompanied everywhere by open-air parties. The spectacle spreads like wildfire from the south to the north and special bulletins – *sakura* (cherry) *zensen* (front) – similar to weather forecasts are issued indicating where exactly the cherry trees will flower. Depending on the location, the period varies from late March to mid to late April and the enchantment lasts just one week. Then the petals fall all at once. The same phenomenon is repeated in cherry bonsai, among the best loved. It is this sudden disappearance, even in a small tree, that appeals so greatly to the Japanese for whom this departure symbolises a clear clean-cut way of leaving life. To produce this extraordinary blossom, *Prunus* x *kanzakura* has had to work hard during the previous spring and summer, laying up abundant reserves of nutrients through the leaves. To obtain this result, the bonsai grower must therefore take great care during the period of maximum activity, providing much more fertiliser and water than for other species. The specimen in the Crespi Bonsai Museum is growing in a fine rectangular Japanese blue glazed *tokoname* pot with rounded corners and no rim.

ENGLISH NAME **Cherry** ❋ ORIGIN **Japan**
❋ AGE **70 years** ❋ HEIGHT **100 cm (39 in)**
❋ HEIGHT IN NATURAL STATE **5-6 m (16-20 ft)**

SPRING

Corylopsis spicata

ENGLISH NAME **Corylopsis**

✤

ORIGIN **Japan**

✤

AGE **80 years**

✤

HEIGHT **100 cm (39 in)**

✤

HEIGHT IN NATURAL STATE **1.8-2.5 m (6-8 ft)**

A native of Japan, in its natural state the winter hazel is a somewhat ramified decorative bush with voluminous foliage and a diameter almost the same as the height. It blossoms at the end of winter, producing a spectacular show of small highly fragrant lemon yellow petals in hanging inflorescences which stand out against the light grey bark and on the leafless branches, giving the plant a particularly feminine gracefulness. The leaves appear immediately afterwards, green in summer then turning golden-yellow in the autumn before falling. From this bushy never particularly tidy species, the refined work of the bonsai master has created a formal upright specimen with layers of well-spaced branches which reveal the full beauty of the *tachiagari*, the first part of the trunk from the base of the tree to the first branch. To obtain generous blossom year after year, the flowers must be removed immediately after 75% have opened. This is the only way to ensure the plant directs its energies to the formation of new leaves and subsequently new flower buds.

SPRING

Rosa banksiae lutea

ENGLISH NAME **Banks' rose**

❋

ORIGIN **Japan**

❋

AGE **60 years**

❋

HEIGHT **83 cm (33 in)**

❋

HEIGHT IN NATURAL STATE **6 m (20 ft)**

Introduced to the West from China in 1825, the thornless Banks' rose enchants for its extraordinary flowering at the beginning of spring, when the long erect but supple shoots are covered with thousands of small light yellow pompom-like flowers in bunches. After so many pink roses, *Rosa banksiae lutea* brings a welcome touch of yellow to the hybrid scene! The resistance of even the tender green leaves to cold is also legendary. In the art of bonsai, it is appreciated for the strength of the naturally rough trunk, enabling it to be shaped into a twisted form which becomes ever more interesting as the years go by. The contrast with the lightness of the shoots and delicacy of the flowers is truly remarkable.

Prunus mume

Known and appreciated since the Edo period (1600-1868), the Japanese apricot is a member of the *Rosaceae* family and was cultivated for the beauty of its white flowers with their delicate honey fragrance. It is the first to blossom during the coldest part of the year when the first petals open up at the end of winter on the leafless branches, before the new leaves emerge. The tree is thus thought to bring good luck and no bonsai collection should be without one! The rough black bark cracks with age and the hard tough wood maintains the signs of ageing over time. The slanting growth and natural fascination of the ancient specimen is shown to best advantage by the fine half-moon stone *mikazuki* pot, although rare and seldom used, the ideal container for the mature bonsai. The half-moon shape is also ideal to emphasise the distinctive characteristics of cascade or semi-cascade bonsai, creating a more balanced union between plant and pot and giving a more natural effect.

ENGLISH NAME **Japanese apricot** ❖ ORIGIN **Japan** ❖ AGE **55 years** ❖ HEIGHT **85 cm (33 in)** ❖ HEIGHT IN NATURAL STATE **5-6 m (16-20 ft)**

Spiraea thunbergii

A native of China but naturalised a long time ago in Japan from where
it was introduced into Europe, *Spiraea thunbergii* is a deciduous
bush and the first of the spireas to blossom in the spring, with a
voluminous mass of small white flowers distributed on the numerous
thin and often pendulous branches. Important for its size, appearance
and personality, half a century of cultivation has accentuated this
bonsai's intrinsic characteristics of lightness. The voluminous foliage
is wonderful and the trunk supports the harmonious and well-defined
layers of vegetation with large well-proportioned empty spaces.
After flowering, the light green lanceolate leaves give the plant a
light harmonious appearance.

ENGLISH NAME **Thunberg spirea** ❊ ORIGIN **Japan** ❊ AGE **50 years**
❊ HEIGHT **70 cm (28 in)** ❊ HEIGHT IN NATURAL STATE **1.5-1.8 m (5-6 ft)**

SPRING

Wisteria floribunda

Inseparably linked to the Japanese tradition, the wisteria, a creeper with a noble elegant appearance whose beauty has enchanted poets since the 8th century in the Heyan period (794-1186), made its entry into the world of the bonsai in the Meji period (1868-1912). A deciduous plant, it flowers at the end of spring with a splendid show of hanging racemes the same length as the inflorescences of the species in the natural state (up to 30 cm [12 in]). The light blue-purple butterfly shaped corollas which open in succession are also the same size. In the small pot, the trunk with imposing base and upright growth habit opens up into a myriad of light shoots, expressing the natural intrinsic force of the creeper. The shoots support light umbrella-shaped foliage made up of compound leaves, formed in turn by 13-19 leaflets with a light tender texture and pale green colour, remaining until late summer.

ENGLISH NAME **Japanese wisteria**

ORIGIN **Japan**

AGE **85 years**

HEIGHT **130 cm (51 in)**

HEIGHT IN NATURAL STATE **More than 10 m (33 ft)**

"Biographies"

Fabio Petroni was born in Corinaldo in the province of Ancona in 1964. He now lives and works in Milan. After studying photography, he collaborated with the most famous professionals in the sector. During his career, he has specialised in portrait and still life photography where he has demonstrated an intuitive rigorous style. Over the years, he has photographed important names from the worlds of culture, medicine and the Italian economy. He works with leading publicity agencies and has put his name to numerous campaigns for prestigious internationally-famous companies. He is directly responsible for the image of a number of important Italian brands. For White Star Publishers he has published *Horses : Master Portraits*, *Mutt's Life!*, *Cocktails*, *Super Cats*, *Roses*, *Chili Pepper : Moments of Spicy Passion*, *Orchids* and *Tea Sommelier*. His website is *www.fabiopetronistudio.com*

Anna Maria Botticelli was born in Genoa and lives in Milan. A biologist and microbiologist by extraction, she has always had a special passion for plants. For more than twenty years she has been collaborating with a number of Italian publishing companies such as Arnoldo Mondadori Editore, Cairo Editore and Periodici San Paolo and is author of a number of features and columns on green themes. She is responsible for the theme of orchids, bonsai and bulbs for "Gardenia," Italy's most important monthly covering flowers, plants and vegetable and flower gardens. She has published *Ritratti di Orchidee* (Portraits of Orchids) (Idealibri, 1990). Together with Clementina Cagnola, herborist and pharmacist, she has written *La salute foglia per foglia* (Health leaf by leaf) (A. Mondadori, 1998). In collaboration with IBC (Netherlands), she was responsible for the technical section of the book *Giardini in vaso* (Pot gardens) (A. Mondadori, 2004). She published *Orchids* (2013) for White Star Publishers. She is author of the Garden Book *I giardini del Negombo* (The Gardens of Negombo) (Grandi Giardini Italiani, 2014).

The author thanks Luigi Crespi, his daughter Susanna Crespi and all the family who made available the Crespi Bonsai Museum bonsai photographed in this book. A special thank you also to bonsai master Nobuyuki Kajiwara and the Crespi Bonsai staff of experts.

After concluding his studies, **Luigi Crespi** became interested in flower growing and his passion for nature and unusual talent earned him a reputation in the world of bonsai and landscaping. Eclectic and with a bent for experimentation, he was the first in Italy to design Japanese gardens. In 1979 he founded Crespi Bonsai and in 1991, the Crespi Bonsai Museum and the Bonsai University. He has written numerous books on bonsai published by leading publishers such as De Agostini, Fabbri and Sperling & Kupfer. During the 1980s, he served an apprenticeship in Japan at the nursery of Shinji Ogasawara, one of the most famous Japanese masters. Since 2006 he has been international consultant of the WBFF World Bonsai Friendship Federation, an international federation promoting bonsai which in 2012 awarded him the WBFF Emeritus Award. In April 2012, the Japanese government awarded him the prestigious "Order of the Rising Sun, Gold and Silver Rays" award for his work in promoting Japanese culture. Since 2013 he has been "Penjing Bonsai Ambassador."

Susanna Crespi, an architecture graduate from Milan Polytechnic, is external relations manager for Crespi Bonsai. She supervises and programmes the courses at the Bonsai University in the various Crespi premises. She organises regular displays, meetings with the most famous Oriental masters, events and exhibitions both in Italy and abroad, including the Crespi Cup International Bonsai Meeting, one of the world's best-known events dedicated to bonsai and suiseki. She is co-founder of Crespi Editori, the publishing company in the Crespi Group whose publications include "BONSAI & news" the sector's most authoritative magazine with the biggest circulation of which she is managing editor. She is editor of books and other publications focussing on various aspects of the art and technique of the bonsai, the art of suiseki, Japanese gardens and plants in general.

"Alphabetical index of bonsai"

"Crespi Bonsai"

The first company to import bonsai into Italy, **Crespi Bonsai** was founded in 1979 by Luigi Crespi when this fascinating art was still practically unknown in Europe. Over the years, Crespi Bonsai has earned itself an international reputation as a prestigious brand, a result achieved partly thanks to the company's profound respect for nature and tradition. Its philosophy has always been to cover every aspect of the bonsai, with rigorous attention to all aspects of this art, from the strictly technical to the aesthetic, culminating in publication of "BONSAI & news," the sector's most authoritative magazine with the biggest circulation. From the Crespi Bonsai Museum to the Bonsai University which proposes short and yearly courses, regular exhibitions including the famous Crespi Cup International Bonsai Meeting and meetings with the most famous Oriental masters, the initiatives are numerous and all with the scope of promoting the art of the bonsai.

The **Crespi Bonsai Museum** which opened in May 1991 was the world's first permanent bonsai museum, born from Luigi Crespi's wish to offer everyone interested in bonsai or wanting to learn more about this culture the possibility of admiring a precious collection including centuries-old trees, fine pots from the Qing, Tokugawa and Meiji periods and antique books.

The Museum structure in concrete and steel combined with natural materials such as slate and Barge stone shows the magnificent specimens on display to best advantage, trees trained by the most famous Japanese masters, such as Kato, Kawamoto, Kaneko, Kawahara and Ogasawara. The most significant pieces in the collection without doubt include the centuries-old *Ficus retusa* located at the centre of a pagoda, its origins lost in the memory of generations of expert bonsai growers. The Crespi Collection includes about two hundred bonsai, displayed on rotation according to the season. This is the most fascinating and extraordinary aspect of the permanent exhibition of living art in the Crespi Bonsai Museum, changing appearance with every season, assuming new colours and becoming ever more perfect as the years go by, thanks to the meticulous care of Luigi Crespi and the improvements introduced by bonsai master Nobuyuki Kajiwara, museum director and lecturer on the three-year courses at the Crespi Bonsai University.

An important position is occupied by the reconstruction of a "toko-no-ma," the alcove in the traditional Japanese home dedicated to displaying objects with a high spiritual content, including bonsai, suiseki and accompanying elements able to immerse the observer in the season.

The collection is completed by precious tansu furniture and various interior design accessories such as ancient Japanese lanterns, while outside the gallery, the gaze can wander among the stones of the zen garden created by Luigi Crespi using original material imported from Japan.

In constant transformation, the precious collection in the Crespi Bonsai Museum is enhanced year after year with fine masterpieces, although it is becoming ever more difficult to acquire new centuries-old specimens, ever more jealously guarded in Japan and China as symbols of traditional culture.

Born in Fukuoka (Japan), bonsai master **Nobuyuki Kajiwara** began teaching the art of bonsai at the Crespi Bonsai University when it was founded in 1991 and since then has also supervised development of the masterpieces in the Crespi Bonsai Museum. Fruit of a lively creative personality refined by a packed curriculum of university studies, his remarkable artistic sensitivity integrates perfectly with a meticulous technique acquired during his apprenticeship with the Kato family (one of Japan's oldest and still practising the art of bonsai today) and above all matured by his experience working and teaching in various countries.

The love and devotion bonsai master Kajiwara dedicates to the specimens in the Crespi Bonsai Museum are evident from the way in which the trees improve season after season, becoming genuine masterpieces of nature.

www.crespibonsai.com

207 *Shohin*, small bonsai of *Malus sp.*, *Celtis sinensis*, *Acer palmatum*, *Acer buergerianum*.
208 *Ginkgo biloba* leaves in autumn.

WS White Star Publishers®
is a registered trademark belonging
to De Agostini Libri S.p.A.

© 2014 De Agostini Libri S.p.A.
Via G. da Verrazano, 15
28100 Novara, Italy
www.whitestar.it - www.deagostini.it

Translation : Arancho Doc

ISBN 978-88-544-0843-2
1 2 3 4 5 6   18 17 16 15 14

Printed in China